Edinburgh Castle's Dog Cemetery

and the stories of

Peter of the Black Watch

Charlie of the Royal Scots

Greyfriars Bobby

and

Pat of the Seaforths

Peter of the Black Watch

In the early 1830's a ship belonging to the Royal Navy called into the Maltese port of Valletta to take on supplies. One of the officers received an invitation to dine with the Black Watch who were stationed on the island and he decided to take his dog along with him.

When the time came for the officer to return to his ship, the Newfoundland refused to leave. Confident that his dog would be well looked after, the officer decided to leave him at the barracks.

The soldiers named the Newfoundland Peter and took up a collection to buy him a collar. The regiment also had a deer mascot and Peter and the stag quickly became good friends. Although both animals were popular with the soldiers, they generally preferred to spend their time with the bandsmen. When the bugler played the call for the regiment to muster for a parade or a route march, the dog and deer joined the band.

As the musicians marched ahead of the regiment wearing

feather bonnets decorated with a red hackle, white tunics and
Royal Stewart tartan kilts, the dog and the deer trotted along at the
front of the band.

Peter reported daily to the cookhouse for his meals plus any
bones that might be available. Except for one bad-tempered cook
Peter usually received a pat on the head and a kind word from the
kitchen staff in addition to his rations.

When the crabbit cook was on duty not only did he refuse to
issue Peter with his rations, he tried to kick him when he turned up
at the cookhouse door. Peter kept out of the bully's way and bided
his time. If the Newfoundland met the cook by accident on the
barrack square, Peter would ignore him, treating him with the
contempt the dog reckoned he deserved.

Being a Newfoundland, Peter was a first-class swimmer. When
the soldiers marched down to the beach to swim in the
Mediterranean, Peter went along to act as lifeguard. The
Newfoundland was always first into the water and last to leave
after the bathers had taken their dip.

One day Peter spotted the cook heading for the beach. Realising that this was the opportunity he had been waiting for, the Newfoundland waded into the water and swam towards the bully.

Fastening his teeth on the cook's leg, Peter dragged him beneath the surface. Fortunately for the cook, his cries for help were heard by a group of soldiers heading for the beach. Swimming to the rescue, they reached the cook just before Peter began to drag him down for the third and final time.

In 1834 the Black Watch sailed for the island of Corfu. A long underground passage led to the entrance of Fort Neuf where the regiment was stationed. Only soldiers who had been issued with a pass to visit the nearby town were allowed to go beyond the fort's boundary.

Reckoning that the regulation also applied to him, Peter would sit on the borderline which lay thirty two yards from the mouth of the tunnel waiting to welcome the soldiers returning from the town. When the bugle sounded he would quickly wheel round and bound back down the tunnel at breakneck speed.

During hot weather the local police patrolled the town in a horse drawn cart rounding up strays. The wagon carried a wooden framed contraption fitted with hooks. When a dog was caught roaming the streets without a collar, the four-footed prisoner was dragged to the cart and hung on the contraption. Peter kept well away from the wagon and the soldiers made every effort to make sure that their mascot did not fall into the dog catchers' hands.

Before taking Peter into town, he was always inspected to make sure he was wearing his collar which was inscribed with the words 'Regimental Dog 42nd Highlanders'. Even although he was not allowed to go into town without it, Peter was nearly picked up by the police on several occasions.

When the Black Watch returned to Scotland in 1836 after serving abroad for nineteen years, the regiment was stationed at Edinburgh Castle. Peter had taken a dislike to one of the officers as he had been mistreated by him. One day as the officer came marching through the gate, the Newfoundland made the mistake of growling at him.

This was the excuse the officer had been waiting for. Showing the Newfoundland no mercy, he gave the order for Peter to be taken away and shot.

The Dog Cemetery

One summer's day in 1847 a funeral procession made its way through Edinburgh Castle. The escort marching behind thirteen year old James MacGregor Grant consisted of four regimental pioneers and two sergeants.

James Grant's father who was an engineer worked at the fortress and the youngster was friendly with the Castle commandant's family. He regularly visited their home in Ramsay Garden which stood on the right hand side of the fort's esplanade. The youngster looked forward to his visits as he could usually count on being treated to a meal in the butler's pantry.

One June morning, James who was on holiday from school decided to pay a visit to the commandant's house. It seemed a long time since he had eaten his morning bowl of porridge and he was feeling famished. Hoping to get a 'tightener' which would see him through till dinner-time, the hungry youngster headed for the commandant's house.

Arriving at the door, James rang the bell. The door was opened by the maid but instead of welcoming him with her usual cheery greeting, she seemed upset and reluctant to let him in. When James asked if anything was wrong, she replied that the family had suffered a sudden bereavement.

The colonel was upstairs in the drawing room. Recognising Jamie's voice he called out to the youngster to come up. Climbing the stairs James found the commandant's wife and two daughters weeping bitterly into their lace handkerchiefs, sobbing "Fido, Fido, poor Fido!"

When James asked if Fido was ill, the colonel replied "Ill my boy? He is worse than that. He is dead! He died this morning at eight o'clock exactly. The assistant surgeon was with him all night and we were all beside him to the last. We did everything that could be done for him, but he died all the same."

James was a pupil at Edinburgh High School. To earn extra money during the holidays, unknown to his parents, he had taken a job as a coffin liner at a funeral parlour on the city's south side. There had been no shortage of work as a cholera epidemic had hit the city but James had been forced to hand in his notice when his mother found a piece of coffin lace while going through his pockets.

Seeing his chances of a square meal flying out the window, James expressed his sympathy and offered to give Fido a decent burial in a quiet spot close to the Castle for a sovereign.

After conferring with his wife and daughters, the commandant decided that the spaniel should be laid to rest in a civilised manner. Handing James a sovereign the officer asked him to handle the arrangements. Pocketing his fee, the youngster borrowed a tape measure from one of the colonel's daughters and tiptoed up to the attic where Fido lay to take the spaniel's measurements.

Assuring the family he had the matter well in hand, James then headed for the Castle. Nodding to the sentry guarding the gate he crossed the drawbridge and made his way to the Armourer's workshop. Handing Fido's measurements to the armourer sergeant, James asked him to instruct the regimental carpenter to knock up a coffin for the spaniel.

The casket was to be lamp black with Fido's name and date of departure painted in white letters on the lid. It was to be lined with white flannel and delivered to the colonel's quarters at three o'clock that afternoon.

James then went to see Corporal Tomkins of the regimental pioneers to arrange for the digging of the grave. The bearded pioneers were the regimental labourers and knew how to use a pick and shovel. Taking the corporal to a small plot below the battery where Mons Meg stood, James pointed to the spot where Fido was to be buried. Using the commandant's authority, James requested that a burial party report to the Armourer's workshop at four o'clock.

At first the corporal refused, highly offended at being asked to act as a pall bearer for a dog, even if he had belonged to the colonel.

He quickly changed his mind when James showed him the sovereign and promised to pay each member of the burial party one shilling.

At four o'clock the funeral party set out from the Armourer's workshop. As the procession consisting of the Barrack Sergeant, the Armourer Sergeant and four regimental pioneers marched over the cobbles of the fortress carrying the coffin, the mourners were targeted by a barrage of insults and cat calls from the soldiers in the fort.

Concentrating on the thought of the shilling they would receive and the pints of beer the money would buy when they had carried out their contract, the pall bearers ignored the insults. Maintaining their dignity the burial party marched steadily on carrying Fido's coffin to its final resting place.

Reaching the spot where Fido was to be buried overlooking West Princes Street Gardens, the soldiers lowered the coffin into the grave and shovelled in the earth. After the sods had been replaced, James handed each of the soldiers a shilling as promised and waved goodbye as they took off at top speed for the Castle's wet canteen.

The regimental adjutant had witnessed the ceremony while carrying out his rounds. When he called on the colonel that evening to deliver his daily report, the officer suggested that the plot which was used as a playground by the garrison's children would make an ideal burial ground for regimental pets who had died in the Castle.

The colonel approved of the adjutant's proposal and suggested that the area should be named the Dog Cemetery. The Fort Major would be responsible for issuing burial permits.

Thirty years later having emigrated to Canada, James returned to the Castle and was surprised to find that forty regimental dogs had been buried in the small plot. The cemetery along with Greyfriars Bobby's drinking fountain which had been erected only a few years previously at the southern end of George IV Bridge was now a favourite spot for tourists visiting the capital.

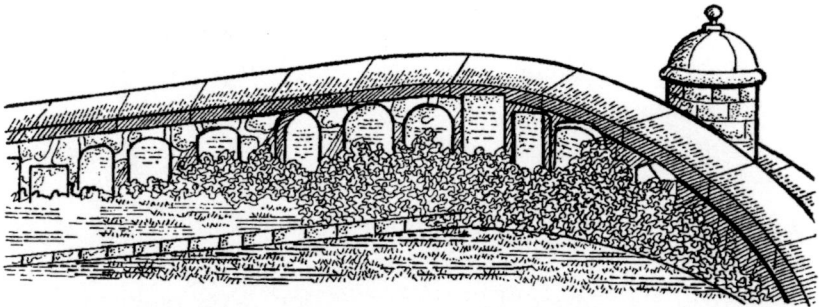

The cemetery was well looked after and a small headstone stood over each grave bearing inscriptions such as 'Frisky, Dog of the 33rd Regiment, served throughout the Crimean War', 'Lions, Dog of the Black Watch, present at Lucknow', 'Caesar, King's Own, present at the Alma'.

Although Fido's resting place has long since disappeared, the spaniel who was the first dog to be buried in the cemetery will never be forgotten.

Charlie of the Royal Scots

In 1853 a small black dog trotted through the gates of Newport Barracks, Monmouthshire, looking for shelter from the freezing winter weather. Although the shaggy-coated stray had an honest intelligent face, he always looked as if he was smiling as he had an oddly shaped mouth.

Five companies of the 1st Battalion Royal Scots were stationed at the barracks. One of the officers had a brilliant set of teeth and always kept his lips apart to show off their sparkling whiteness. As soon as the soldiers spotted the little black mongrel grinning at them from the corner of the parade ground they nicknamed him 'Charlie' after the officer.

For the first few days Charlie sat at the edge of the parade ground watching the soldiers going about their duties, practising drill and forming up for parade.

There was no shortage of four-footed pets in the barracks. Every day when the regimental surgeon left his quarters to inspect the sick parade, he found a pack of dogs waiting outside his door. Not long after Charlie's arrival as the surgeon headed for the hospital, he spotted the little dog and gave him a nod and a friendly greeting. Assuming that he had been invited to join the pack, the little mongrel fell in behind the four-footed column.

The surgeon's first duty was to examine soldiers reporting sick that morning. Following the doctor into the surgery, Charlie positioned himself so that he could get a good look at each man as he came in to be examined.

As each soldier explained his symptoms to the doctor, Charlie looked them and up and down from head to toe as if he had been called in to give a second opinion. The little dog looked from the soldier to the surgeon with an air of professional concern as the doctor examined his patient.

After examining the sick parade, the doctor began his tour of the hospital wards. As the surgeon went from room to room checking the patients, Charlie trotted behind, stopping at each bed like a visiting consultant. When the doctor finished his rounds, Charlie escorted him back across the parade ground to his quarters.

The little black mongrel carried out the same routine every day.

Although Charlie was popular with everyone from the company cooks to the colonel, he remained totally independent. He also refused to mix with the other dogs which often resulted in a bloody battle. After one fierce fight Charlie was so badly injured that he had to be carried to the hospital and fitted with a set of splints.

Although Charlie now had trouble getting around he did not neglect his duties. Hopping along on three legs, he regularly turned up for his hospital appointments until his splints were removed and he was taken off the sick list.

In 1854 as it looked as if Russia planned to invade Turkey, the British, French, and Turkish governments decided to send a military force to the Crimea. The British force commanded by Lord Raglan consisted of 27,000 officers and men.

When the Royal Scots first battalion commanded by Major Montgomery consisting of 30 officers, 46 sergeants, 15 drummers, 850 rank and file plus 28 soldiers' wives marched up the gang plank of the *S.S. Oude* at Plymouth in March, Charlie led them aboard.

After leaving Gibraltar as the overcrowded vessel steamed past the Rock of Galatea at midday on 29th April a fire broke out in the ship's engine room. Fearing that the fire would spread to the magazine which was packed with ammunition, the steamship's captain gave orders for the boxes to be thrown overboard.

Working quickly and efficiently the soldiers and crew carried the wooden crates containing over 47,000 rounds of ammunition from the magazine and dropped them into the sea, supervised by Charlie and the officers. The rounds of ammunition were replaced when the steamship arrived at Malta to take on coal and supplies.

Arriving at the Turkish port of Gallipoli on 4th May, the battalion was assigned to the first brigade of the third division. A few days later the officers and men left the cemetery where they had been ordered to set up camp and headed for the town of Cheflik which lay three miles from the port.

At Cheflik the battalion took part in manoeuvres to prepare for the coming campaign.

Colonel Bell commander of the second battalion which was stationed at Cephalonia in the Ionian Islands arrived to take over command of the first at the end of the month.

Not long after his arrival the battalion was hit by an outbreak of dysentery. Charlie also caught the bug. Although the little mongrel was as tough as nails, he quickly began to slide downhill.

Too weak to walk, Charlie crawled into the surrounding fields. Finding a plant which would cure him, Charlie chewed the green leaves. The herbal remedy worked and the little dog soon recovered his stamina. Back on his own four feet, Charlie resumed his regimental duties. As regular as clockwork he trotted round the camp inspecting the tents and visiting the sick.

On 20th June the battalion was ordered to return to Gallipoli. On their way the Royal Scots passed a French division also heading for the Turkish port to embark for the Crimea. The French regimental bands played 'God Save the Queen' as the Royal Scots marched past. The red coated infantrymen returned the musical

salute with shouts of of "Vive L'Empereur!"

Armed now with the new Minié rifle instead of Brown Bess muskets, the battalion sailed from Gallipoli. Landing at Varna in Bulgaria on 26th June the battalion set up camp on the outskirts of the Black Sea port.

Charlie had no shortage of patients to visit as the regiment was hit by a cholera epidemic the following month. Although the battalion moved to the heights of Galata to escape the outbreak, twenty six men died of the terrible disease.

At the end of August the Royal Scots received orders to join the allied invasion force. The regiment including Charlie embarked for the Crimea on the troopship *Alfred the Great.*

The invasion fleet arrived at Calamita Bay on 14th September. Ordered to leave their knapsacks on board, each man packed his sleeping blanket, spare shirt, pair of boots and socks inside his greatcoat before rolling it up and slinging it over his left shoulder. Each soldier was issued with three days' rations consisting of biscuits and pork plus fifty rounds of ammunition.

Darkness had fallen by the time Charlie and the battalion landed on the beach. The rain was coming down in buckets and although the men were wearing greatcoats, they were quickly soaked to the skin by the torrential downpour.

By morning the weather had improved and the rain had stopped falling. The soldiers' greatcoats were drenched and their dark grey trousers caked with mud. Detachments were sent out to look for driftwood to build a fire. Finding a wreck lying on the beach the soldiers stripped the wood from the stranded vessel.

The allied force now numbered 65,000 men. The colours of each regiment were removed from their covers and unfurled. Led by their military bands, the British, French and Turkish troops began the march south towards the Russian naval base at Sevastopol.

To prevent the allies reaching the port, a Russian force consisting of 3,600 cavalry and 36,000 infantry commanded by Prince Mentschikoff took up a defensive position on a range of hills behind the River Alma.

As the French troops were stationed on the right of the allied attack they were supported by the fleet's guns. The third division which included the Royal Scots formed part of the right brigade's reserve. Crossing the river, as the British infantry advanced with the cavalry protecting their flank through the vineyards lying at the foot of the hills, the soldiers were targeted by the Russian guns.

Dodging the cannonballs as they bounced along the ground towards him, Charlie quickly learned to survive by taking cover behind bushes and rocks. After three hours hard fighting the Russians were forced to retreat.

As the allies marched south towards Sevastopol, Charlie would leave the column to search for rabbits. Although the little dog occasionally got lost, he had no trouble finding his way back as he could spot the soldiers' red coats even if the column was miles away. No matter how far he roamed when out hunting, Charlie always managed to catch up with the column's rear guard.

Crossing the River Katchka and the River Belbec the allied army continued the march to Sevastopol. As the massive granite forts on the town's northern side were protected by heavy artillery, it was decided to march round the harbour and camp on the high ground to the south.

In addition to being protected by the guns of the Black Sea fleet anchored in the harbour, the Russians were not short of heavy artillery and ammunition as the town contained a massive arsenal.

The high ground occupied by the British force sloped gradually down to the besieged town and varied in height from 500 to 1,000 feet. Armed with picks and shovels the soldiers began digging trenches. The Royal Scots were assigned to the section of the line stretching to the steep cliffs of Picket House Ravine.

Charlie usually accompanied the convoy when the horse drawn wagons were sent to pick up supplies from the port of Balaclava which lay six miles from the British trenches. In addition to his other duties the little dog continued to carry out his weekly inspection of the camp. As he trotted round the lines, in addition to taking a look inside the soldiers' tents, Charlie checked the military hospital.

On 5th November supported by heavy artillery and taking advantage of a thick fog to cover their advance, two columns consisting of nearly 30,000 Russian troops marched out of Sevastopol at dawn to mount a surprise attack on the British positions.

Quickly assembling a force of 374 officers and men, Colonel Bell left the trenches and marched at top speed to reinforce the Light Division on Victoria Ridge. The ridge which lay parallel to Inkerman Ridge consisted of steep rocky spurs jutting out at right angles divided by long deep ravines.

Moving as fast as the rugged terrain would allow, the Royal Scots crossed a rocky gully towards Victoria Ridge and took up position in a Russian artillery battery.

The Russians mounted an attack to retake the strategically important position now occupied by the Royal Scots. Spotting the grey coated columns advancing with bugles blowing and fixed bayonets, Colonel Bell sent two companies into the deep gullies on either side of the battery to protect his flanks.

Supported by heavy artillery, the Russian infantrymen fought desperately with rifle and bayonet to drive the Royal Scots from the position. Although the Russians received reinforcements, the outnumbered redcoats fought like demons forcing the enemy to retreat.

In addition to receiving the C.B., Colonel Bell was mentioned in dispatches. Charlie also received an award. The little black dog was presented with a brass collar inscribed with the title 'Royal Charlie'. He also received a medal inscribed with the names of the battles he had taken part in.

Fiercely proud of his campaign medal, Charlie made sure that his 'gong' got noticed as he trotted around the camp. If the soldiers did not pay his decoration the attention he thought it deserved, Charlie would sit waiting patiently until he received due recognition.

On November 18th the area around Sevastopol was hit by a hurricane. The tremendous storm lasted twelve hours, uprooting the soldiers' bell tents and blowing them out to sea.

The supply depot at Balaclava was severely hit, while the road linking the port with the trenches was now practically impassable as it had been turned into a swamp by the torrential rain. Twenty one supply ships anchored in the harbour containing clothing, medicines, rations and ammunition were wrecked, while eight had been damaged by the storm.

In the trenches the soldiers found themselves not only short of food and ammunition but knee deep in mud. Exposed to enemy fire, the officers and men faced the winter without adequate clothing as the uniforms they had landed in were now ragged and torn. By the end of the month 8,000 British soldiers had been hospitalised.

In April the following year when the Royal Scots second battalion arrived at Balaclava the officers and men were brigaded with the first. On 11th August Private Prosser of the second battalion won the Victoria Cross when he left the trenches to help carry a wounded soldier to safety under heavy enemy fire.

On 8th September although a force including the Royal Scots first battalion mounted an attack on Sevastopol's Redan bastion the infantry were driven back.

The following day the allies found that the Redan was deserted as the Russians had evacuated Sevastopol by constructing a pontoon bridge and retreating to the opposite side of the harbour.

Following the capture of the Russian fort, Charlie's medal and collar were taken away for cleaning and repair. Mistaking the little dog for a stray, Charlie was picked up by a soldier from another regiment who sold him to an officer for ten shillings.

Under the impression that the dog had been captured from the enemy, the officer tied a piece of string round Charlie's neck and headed back to his quarters, but as soon as Charlie was released he took off like a bullet for his own regiment.

While levelling the earthworks in front of the Redan, Charlie and a corporal were supervising a working party. At midday the corporal announced it was time for a break. Stopping work the soldiers laid down their picks and shovels and went into an ammunition store.

After they had eaten their pork and biscuits, Charlie and the corporal popped outside for a breath of fresh air. Inside the store one of the privates took out his pipe to have a smoke. A spark fell on the floor. Although the magazine was empty, the floor was saturated with gunpowder.

The ammunition store exploded instantly, the tremendous blast killing the seven privates, while Charlie and the corporal who were standing outside were blown off their feet. Although the corporal who now resembled a chimney sweep was severely

shocked and Charlie was singed from nose to tail, they both survived the hair raising experience.

In 1856 when the Royal Scots were stationed at Aldershot, the Crimean veterans were reviewed by Queen Victoria. As the monarch accompanied by her husband Prince Albert, the Duke of Cambridge and an escort consisting of high ranking officers rode along the red coated ranks, the Queen was amused to see Charlie perched on the shoulders of a giant grenadier standing close to the regimental colours.

The following year the first battalion received orders to sail for India. As the regimental band played on the docks and the crowds waved farewell, the Royal Scots marched up the troopship's gangplank with the little black mongrel at their head.

Greyfriars Bobby

In 1861 a time gun was installed on Edinburgh Castle's Half Moon Battery. At one o'clock every day except on Sundays and public holidays, the exact time was transmitted electrically from the Royal Observatory on the Calton Hill along an overhead wire over 4,000 feet long to the fortress.

Colour Sergeant Donald MacNab Scott worked in the Castle's workshops. The sergeant lived in lodgings at 28 Candlemaker Row. The building's rear windows looked out on to the burial ground of Greyfriars Kirk. Three years before the time gun had been set up a small dog had appeared in the Greyfriars area. The locals called the dog Bobby.

The colour sergeant became friends with Bobby and treated him regularly to a meal at restaurants in the area including Currie's Eating House which stood close to the church in Greyfriars Place.

The *Inverness Advertiser* featured the story of Bobby in 1864. The story was picked up by other papers including *The Scotsman* and the Greyfriars Bobby legend began.

Five years later Angela Burdett-Coutts who was a member of the Ladies' Committee of the R.S.P.C.A. travelled up to Edinburgh with her friend Hannah Brown to see the little dog now under the Lord Provost's protection.

On a cold November day accompanied by some friends Angela visited Greyfriars to see the dog who had been trained by Colour Sergeant Scott to turn up for his dinner when the One o'clock Gun went off.

When she enquired who the dog had belonged to, Angela was told that Bobby had been owned by an Army veteran called Robert Gray. After Robert had died in the Royal Infirmary, Bobby had begun inhabiting Greyfriars kirkyard. Reaching the spot where the dog's owner was said to have been buried Angela and her friends found that the grave was unmarked.

Returning to her suite in the Balmoral Hotel in Princes Street, Angela immediately wrote a letter to the Town Council asking for permission to set up a headstone.

Angela received a reply stating that the Council would consider the request, but the information she had been given on who the dog had belonged to would have to be checked out. The gravestone was never erected.

Crowds gathered daily outside the church to see Bobby trot out through the gates at one. When Colour Sergeant Scott set off for the Castle, the little dog would follow him to the end of George IV Bridge before returning to the area he knew best.

Colour Sergeant Scott was discharged from the Army in 1866. The following year when Bobby was having his portrait painted by Gourlay Steell in the artist's studio, the time gun fired as usual at one. When he heard the bang Bobby began to get excited and refused to settle down until he had been given his dinner.

Angela was made a baroness in 1871. Baroness Burdett-Coutts had not forgotten Bobby and although she had been unable to persuade the Town Council to erect a headstone for Robert Gray, she wrote again asking for permission to donate a memorial of Bobby to the city.

Receiving permission, Angela arranged for a drinking fountain to be designed. A red granite fountain was erected in front of a lampost at the south end of George IV Bridge just across from Greyfriars Kirk's main gate. In addition to a metal cup attached to a chain for the use of passers by, dogs were able to drink from the fountain as the pedestal's base was shaped like a trough.

A full-size bronze statue of Bobby sculpted by William Brodie R.S.A. stood on top of the pedestal. The memorial was unveiled in November 1873 and Baroness Burdett-Coutts was given the freedom of the city the following year.

Although he had been born in Perth, Colour Sergeant Scott continued to live in Edinburgh until the end of his days. The Royal Engineer who had become part of the Greyfriars Bobby legend died at the city's Royal Infirmary.

Pat of the Seaforths

As Major General Roberts focussed his binoculars on the Asmai Heights in Afghanistan he spotted a group of infantrymen accompanied by a small white dog engaged in a battle with Afghan tribesmen.

Afghanistan lay between Russia and India. In 1878 when news was received that the Czar was planning to invade India via Afghanistan, a British force commanded by General Roberts was sent through the Khyber Pass to warn the Russians off.

After defeating the Afghans, the military force occupied the Sherpore cantonment which lay outside the capital Kabul. The following year as the occupation force showed no signs of leaving 100,000 tribesmen joined forces to drive the British troops back through the Khyber Pass.

A force of Afghan tribesmen occupied the Asmai Heights which lay not far from Kabul. To protect the capital, Brigadier General Baker was ordered to march against the tribesmen with a force of 1,600 men. The general's brigade consisted of detachments from the Bengal Lancers, 72nd Highlanders, Gordon Highlanders and two Indian Army regiments.

The Highlanders were armed with single shot breech loading Martini-Henry rifles while the Indian troops carried Sniders. Supported by four mountain guns, General Baker's brigade split the Afghan force in two by capturing a pass not far from the Aliabad Kotal.

The brigade which included Pat a small white dog who belonged to one of the 72nd's officers now sheltered from the scorching heat in the village of Bilan Khel waiting for the order to advance up the rocky shale covered slopes against the tribesmen.

The artillerymen had positioned their guns to cover the pass. Loading the 7 pounders, the gunners began shelling an enemy fort which lay nearly a mile away. Led by a tribal chief mounted on a brown horse, the Afghans suddenly charged from the fort towards the mountain gun battery.

Carrying brightly coloured flags and armed with swords, knives and muskets, the tribesmen advanced at top speed towards the battery, their war cries echoing off the mountain sides. Realising they were about to be over run, the battery commander ordered his men to dismantle the guns and pack them on the mules. The artillery officer had underestimated the speed of the Afghan charge and the tribesmen were almost upon them.

A company of the 72nd including Pat had been ordered up the pass to clear a group of Afghans from the ridge. Spotting that the gunners were in trouble, Captain Spens and a colour sergeant led the Highlanders and a company of Sikh infantry to help them out. Lance Corporal Sellar and Pat were first to reach the tribesmen.

While the lance corporal fought the Afghans off with his rifle and bayonet, Pat sunk his teeth into a tribesman's leg. Although Captain Spens managed to run an Afghan through with his broadsword, he was killed by a single stroke from the tribesman's razor sharp knife.

General Baker sent his Indian troops to drive the Afghans back, but the tribesmen who had captured two of the mountain guns forced them to retreat. After being reinforced by troops from

Kabul, the guns were recaptured and escorted back to the city by the Bengal Lancers.

General Roberts had witnessed the hand to hand fight on the ridge through his field glasses and he recommended Lance Corporal Sellar who like Pat had been wounded for the Victoria Cross.

In 1881 the 72nd Duke of Albany's Own Highlanders amalgamated with the 78th (Ross-shire Buffs) to form the Seaforth Highlanders. After being stationed in Aden, the regiment's first battalion was sent to Egypt where Pat took part in the Battle of Tel-el-Kebir.

Every year to commemorate the courage Pat had shown during the Afghan War, the lance corporal's Victoria Cross was attached to the little dog's collar.

When the Seaforths returned to Scotland at the beginning of 1886, the regiment was stationed at Edinburgh Castle barracks. Pat died two years later and was buried in the Dog Cemetery. The little dog's obituary was published in *The Scotsman*.

Headstones in the Dog Cemetery

1. Obliterated

2. Ranger, Loving friend of Col. and Mrs Dugg 1898-1907

3. Brig. and Mrs. Cunningham, Tippy Top, age 16, July 17th 1940

4. Amber, 18th November 1953, Owner Lt. Col. Neville Blair,
   The Black Watch

5. Billy, The pet of a Gordon Highlander, Died 20th October 1906

6. Winkle, Dear and faithful friend of Lady Gow and the
   Governor, Died 1980.

7. In memory of Flora, canteen pet of the Royal Scots,
   Died 7th February 1885

8. In memory of Chips (obliterated)

9. Topsy. The Drs. pet (obliterated) Royal Scots

10. & 11. Both headstones obliterated

12. Sheena, friend and companion for 13 years in Germany,
    Singapore and Scotland. Died September 1962

13. Flora, the band pet, 79th Q.O.C. 1.10.76

14. General Sir William Peyton's Tinker, died 1935.

15. Obliterated

16. In memory of Pat who followed the 72nd Highlanders
    in P (obliterated) for 10 years, died 1888

17. Scamp, faithful chum of Jack Wilson Patterson, 1947